This book is due for return on or before the last date shown below.

Mother Teresa

THE APOSTLE OF LOVE

Copyright © Rupa & Co 2002
Text © 2002 Gautam Ghosh

First Published 2002
Second impression 2004

Published by

Rupa & Co

7/16, Ansari Road, Daryaganj,
New Delhi 110 002

Sales Centres:

Allahabad Bangalore Chandigarh Chennai
Hyderabad Jaipur Kathmandu Kolkata
Ludhiana Mumbai Pune

Photographs courtesy: Indranil Seal & Photo Division

Cover & Book Design by
Arrt Creations
45 Nehru Apts, Kalkaji,
New Delhi 110 019

Printed in India by
Gopsons Papers Ltd.,
A-14 Sector 60
Noida-201301

Mother Teresa

THE APOSTLE OF LOVE

Gautam Ghosh

Rupa & Co

CONTENTS

CHAPTER ONE

The Early Years

The third amongst the four Indian nationals who have received the Nobel Prize till date, Mother Teresa was, however, not born in India.

Born Gonxha Bojaxhiu in Skopje, Macedonia on August 26, 1910, she was the youngest of the three children of the Albanian couple Nikolle and Drandafille Bojaxhiu. While her father was a successful businessman, a well-known contractor, who also had business interest in a food shop, her mother was a simple housewife. Her father travelled a lot and knew quite a few languages.

In 1910, Skopje was under the Ottoman Empire and most of the Albanians there were Muslims. However, the Bojaxhius were devout Catholics, who prayed every evening, went to the church regularly and assisted in the service for the Holy Virgin. They were generous people — they cared for the poor and the needy who knocked on their doors, with warmth and generosity. Her father taught her the first lessons in charity and her mother, who looked after an alcoholic

The young Agnes Gonxha Bojaxhiu

lady and another widow with six children, imbibed in her the spirit of 'love thy neighbour as you would love Me.' These early experiences left a lasting impact on young Gonxha's mind, and, later on, in many of her now famous speeches, she would often quote St. John as saying 'You are a liar if you say you love God and you don't love your neighbour. How can you love God whom you do not see, if you do not love your neighbour whom you see, whom you touch, with whom you live?'

Mother Teresa felt that August 27, 1910, the day she was baptised and christened as Agnes Gonxha Bojaxhiu, was her true birthday.

The young Agnes liked to read, pray, sing, and spend her time in the church. She also helped her mother with her social work. She was a soprano, and together with her eldest sister Aga, she was in the church choir.

In 1919, when Agnes was only nine years old, her father suddenly expired, and it fell on her mother to raise her three children all on her own. Her mother stitched wedding dresses and did embroidery, but also took timeout for her children's education. Of the three Bojaxhiu children, Lazar won a scholarship in Austria, Aga followed to a commercial school and Agnes went to Lyceum, a Roman Catholic elementary school.

It was while attending school that she first felt that she had a vocation to help the poor, and desired to spend her life for

Ottoman Empire in 1912

7

God's work. She was just twelve then, and like any young girl of her age would be, was not sure if God really wanted her to choose such a life. So she asked the priest to whom she used to confess in the church, and he answered that 'she could be sure through her joy - the deep inner joy is the compass that indicates the direction of life.'

While still in her teens, Agnes joined 'Sodality', a group of young people from her local parish. Her involvement with the activities of the group developed in her a keen interest in the work of missionaries. She started assisting in several religious activities at Letnice, a pilgrimage place where she had spent several holidays with her parents, and soon made up her mind to become a nun. On September 25, 1928, at the age of just 18, she left Skopje for Ireland where she entered the Order of the Sisters of Our Lady of Loreto, a community known for their missionary work in India.

Before leaving Macedonia, Agnes visited Letnice to pray to Our Lady for her blessings for her life's mission. She travelled across Zagreb to Austria, then to Switzerland, France, London, and finally to the abbey close to Dublin where the motherhouse of the Loreto sisters was. At the abbey she learned to speak in English, and was trained in the religious life. When she took her vows as a Sister of

Loreto, she chose the humble Therese of Lisieux, as her patron Saint. She had stopped at Lisieux on her way to Dublin. But another sister of the Order had already adopted that name, and so, to avoid confusion, the spelling "Teresa" was accepted.

After a few months' training in Dublin, she started her journey for India, her dream destination. It was in the month of December of 1928, that she accompanied a group of sisters on this long and tiring journey. They spent that Christmas singing Christmas carols on the ship. She reached Calcutta via Colombo and Madras, and proceeded to Darjeeling, where she was to continue her

training towards her religious vows. Soon after, she was sent back to Calcutta, the capital of Bengal, to teach at a school for girls.

In Calcutta, Sister Teresa taught geography and catechism (teaching through questions and answers) at St. Mary's High School. Here she taught till 1946, and had become the Principal in 1944. In 1946, Sister Teresa became very ill and was unable to continue teaching. She was suspected of having contracted tuberculosis, and was sent to Darjeeling for rest and recuperation.

It was on the train to Darjeeling that Sister Teresa received "the call within the call" from God "to be God's Love in action to the poorest of the poor." The date was September 10, 1946, and the 'call' entailed that she leave the convent and work with the poor. In her own words, "I realised that I had the call to take care of the sick and the dying, the hungry, the naked, the homeless..." and that "I knew where I belonged, but I did not know how to get there." The 10th of September is thus a landmark date in Sister Teresa's life, and it is still remembered as "Inspiration Day."

Sister Teresa did not hesitate for a moment, but asked permission to leave the Loreto congregation and to establish a new order of sisters. She was then only 36 years old and an European, and India was about to become independent, so the Archbishop of Calcutta told Sister to postpone her decision for atleast a year and instead join the Daughters of Saint Anna and work among the poor. But Sister Teresa was not happy with this response. She renewed her request again after a year. This time the archbishop understood her, but decided to ask the permission from the Vatican and from the Mother General of her order in Dublin. This decision took a long time, and it was only in August 1948 that the Vatican granted Sister Teresa the permission to leave the Sisters of Loreto and pursue her calling under the jurisdiction of the Archbishop of Calcutta.

Sister Teresa chose a simple white saree with sapphire blue bands, representing God's Will, as her Order's attire. She understood that she could help the poor who lived in a dirty environment by learning to prevent and cure sickness. Thus, medical training was indispensable for the fulfillment of her new calling. She therefore joined the nurses training course held at the hospital run by Mother Dengel and her Medical Missionary Sisters in Patna.

It was a simple beginning for her new order. She returned to Calcutta after four months and started working and living in the only slum with which she was acquainted, located just behind St. Mary's High School. Sister Teresa went into the homes of the sick to treat them. The poor were surprised at the dedicated service of the

Mother House at 54A, Lower Circular Road, Kolkata

European lady in an ordinary saree, speaking fluent Bengali. Sister helped them wash, clean and care for themselves, and she soon began to teach the poor children to read and write, and about hygiene. Later on, she found a place to open a school for them, where all the attending children received a cup of milk and a piece of soap. They also learnt about God who really loved them.

In 1949, some of Sister Teresa's former pupils joined her order. The first to join was a Bengali girl from a well-to-do family who came to stay with Sister and work with her. Sister explained to her the vagaries of her vocation and asked her to wait for some time and think it over. The girl went back, but returned on 19th March 1949 to join Sister. She took Sister's childhood name, Agnes and then many others followed.

The sisters woke up early in the morning, prayed for a long time to find the spiritual strength to do the menial work in the service of the poor. One of the basic vows that the sisters took was that they devoted themselves out of their free will, and out of love for Jesus, to the service of the poorest of the poor. This was their chosen way to live and spread the gospel, and work for the salvation of the poor. During their work they found men, women and children dying on the streets, and in order to care for these helpless people, the group rented a room.

Soon the community grew, and Sister Teresa started thinking seriously about starting a congregation. She asked Father Julien Henry s.j. and Father Celest Van Exem s.j. for help and advice in writing out the first "Constitution of the Society of the Missionaries of Charity," which was presented to the Archbishop of Calcutta to be sent to Rome for approval.

In 1950, Sister Teresa adopted Indian nationality, and in the autumn of that year itself Pope Pius XII approved the constitution of the MISSIONARIES OF CHARITY. On 7th of October 1950, the day of

the Feast of the Holy Rosary, the foundation of the Missionaries of Charity was celebrated in the chapel of the sisters. The archbishop celebrated mass, and Father Van Exem read the foundation papers.

On that day, there were 12 sisters. Within five years, the congregation was recognised as a pontifical congregation under the direct jurisdiction of Rome.

While the number of poor and sick that asked for help was increasing by the day, the admiration for the work of the devoted sisters was also growing. A bigger accommodation to accept the increasing number of sisters became a necessity. The solution came after a Novena to St. Cecilia, when a Muslim leaving Calcutta for Pakistan sold his big house to the Missionaries for a cheap price, and this became the famous Mother House at 54A, Lower Circular Road (now known as Acharya Jagadish Chandra Bose Road) in Calcutta.

CHAPTER TWO

Missionary Of Charity

Mother Teresa considered leaving the Congregation of Our Lady of Loreto as the biggest sacrifice in her life. She had suffered the pain of separation when she had left her family, and her country, to go to the convent where she was transformed spiritually and became a nun. But she considered the Congregation as her second family, also loved the work that she was assigned to do by the Congregation at St. Mary's High School in Calcutta. Therefore, when she finally left the Convent on 16th August 1948, she experienced a strong feeling of loss that seemed difficult to overcome.

The day before she left her convent, the feast commemorating the Assumption into heaven of Mary, the mother of Jesus, was held. Mother Teresa wanted it that way, as the feast exalted the ideals that she was striving to achieve in her new life. The following day, she left the convent without her religious habit, for the first time in 18 years. She hardly made it to the middle of the street, when she was overcome with fear of the uncertainties facing her in her new life — she was completely alone, had no place to stay, nothing to eat, no savings and no work. Yet she was still a nun, and committed to God by vows of poverty, chastity and obedience, and most of all, she had received the "command" to "serve the poorest of the poor."

She had to plan her own future. First she had to choose a habit for her order, and, in keeping with the lifestyle she chose, to literally live out the life of the poorest of the poor that she was to serve. She chose a simple white saree, with blue bands on the border, and sandals. The poor that she was to serve were mostly sick, covered with sores and often infected with leprosy. They urgently needed medical care. So she took up a nursing course in Patna. Though initially she had even taken to eating just rice and salt, like the poor that she was to serve, soon she was persuaded that if she continued eating like that, then she would waste away and die

like the impoverished and would not be able to serve them. She therefore decided to eat simple food, but sufficiently, so that she could remain in good health and thus dedicate herself to serving the poor.

On returning to Calcutta, she decided to set up home in the slum located behind St. Mary's High School. A woman rented out to her a miserable shack for five Rupees a month, and that was her first home. Her work began the very next day when she found five children to teach the first letters of the Bengali alphabet, tracing them on the dirty floor with a stick. Her life had changed so radically.

A few months earlier, she was the principal of the famous school just across the street, teaching daughters of rich families; and now she was teaching the children of the poor in a shack in a slum, where people lived in misery among mosquitoes and rats. The paths between the shacks served as open sewers, and the heat was suffocating. Mother Teresa's clothes clung to her sweating body and the children's heads were full of lice. The contrast was severe, and the change extremely difficult to adjust to. But Mother Teresa had chosen that life on her own volition and she was determined to persevere. Mother Teresa did not have time to ponder. The number of her students increased from five on the first day to 25 three days later, and soon to 41. Soon she started visiting the

Kalighat temple

labyrinths of the squalid slums of Calcutta. She went from one shack to the other, from one hut to the next, and tried to help the people living in them. She encountered stark misery and suffering, and came across the blind, the crippled, lepers, people with disfigured faces and deformed bodies, people who could not stand upright and followed her on all fours for a little food.

One day, she came across a woman lying half-dead in a heap of rubbish. She took her to the hospital, but they initially refused to take her in, as they couldn't do anything for her. It was only on her protests and insistence that they took her in, and the woman was saved. Afterwards, thanking Mother for what she had done for her, the woman confessed that it was her son who had thrown her into the garbage. At that time, there were about a million homeless people in Calcutta.

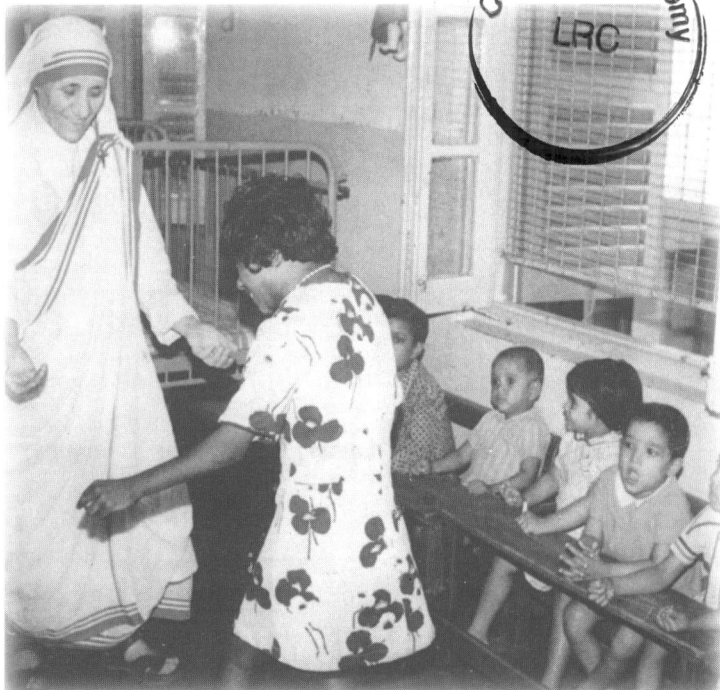

From the hospital, Mother went straight to the municipal authorities of Calcutta and asked for a place where she could take in these dying people. She was taken to the abandoned *dharamshala* adjacent to the famous Kalighat temple, where earlier the pilgrims used to rest after they worshipped the goddess. The building was empty, and when she was offered it, she happily accepted. Within 24 hours, the 'Home for the Dying Destitutes' started functioning.

The year was 1952, and NIRMAL HRIDAY, or Pure Heart, as she had named the 'Home of the Dying Destitutes' in Calcutta, was the first of the fifty-odd projects of the Missionaries of Charity in India. Mother Teresa and her nuns would gather the dying from the streets of Calcutta, bring them to the 'Home', clean them and dress them up in fresh clothes, put them into bed, give them medical attention, and take care of them till their death. Thousands of people have since been transported to the 'Home', where half of them died in a humane environment. In their last hours or days, they received love and compassion and could feel that they were also children of God. Those who lived on were either resettled or sent to other homes where they could live happily for some more time. It is said that Mahatma Gandhi had once cleaned this same building, and had expressed his desire of some holy person taking it over and using it for the good of the Harijan or God's People. Mother Teresa's opening the 'Home' here, in a way, fulfilled Gandhiji's wish.

Mother Teresa's arms were always stretched to receive the unwanted and the uncared for children. No matter how a child reached her,

she never refused one, and each one of them was loved and cared for. SHISHU BHAVAN or the 'Home for the Child' was another early foundation of Mother Teresa and her Missionaries of Charity. Many of the children there have parents who cannot care for them, and therefore do not want them. Mother or her nuns themselves had picked up some of them, while others are brought there from hospitals, prisons and the police. Some of these children who grew up in these homes, got educated and have themselves become messengers of love.

Another category of the downtrodden people that Mother Teresa took special care of are the lepers. Mother visualised her Jesus in every human being, and felt that in washing the lepers' wounds, she was actually nursing the Lord himself. However, the position of the lepers was appalling. They were banned from society, and lived and died like animals. Traditionally, people thought that the disease was a punishment from God, and hence one had to accept the disease and suffer without complaint.

Mother Teresa explained that this was a disease that, in most cases, could be cured. She utilised a fallow piece of land beside the railway station, and in 1957 started a colony there, where the lepers could live and work in peace. She named this colony SHANTI

NAGAR or colony of peace. The lepers here build their own bamboo houses and till their own land. They also weave the bandages for their wounds, and make their own clothes. The person in charge of this colony is an Albanian doctor who joined the Missionaries of Charity.

Mother Teresa would humbly admit that the Missionaries of Charity was not an organisation of social workers, but something more. They gave more than just taking care of the sick. The aim of the Missionaries of Charity was to bring God's love to the people by their service, and they realised that they learnt the real meaning of loving and serving God from the poor people themselves. She believed that the poor gave much more than what they received and would often say, "When a poor person dies of hunger, it has not happened because God did not take care of him or her, it has happened because neither you nor I wanted to give that person what he or she needed."

Like the Hindu monk Swami Vivekananda, who promulgated the theory of finding God amongst all beings, Mother Teresa found Jesus disguised as 'the dying, the cripple, the unwanted and the unloved.' And again, like Swami Vivekananda's *guru* Sri Ramakrishna, Mother would say, "There is only one God, and He is God to all; therefore it is important that everyone is seen as equal before God. I've always said we should help a Hindu become a better Hindu, a Muslim become a better Muslim, a Catholic become a better Catholic. We believe our work should be our example to people. We have among us 475 souls — 30 families are Catholics and the rest are all Hindus, Muslims, Sikhs — all different religions. But they all come to our prayers."

CHAPTER THREE

Love Until it Hurts

Mother Teresa was a great believer in the power of prayer and meditation, and she and her sisters woke up early in the morning and prayed for a long time to find the spiritual strength to do the work in the service of the poor. Mother also indulged in community prayers, known as *litanies*, to invoke God and beg of Him for a grace or a gift, and whenever she needed a special favour or faced any difficulties, she would do an *Express Novena*, that is nine Memoraries in a row.

'Love till it hurts'

Mother would say, 'Before you speak, it is necessary for you to listen, for God speaks in the silence of the heart', and solemnised this in the prayer:

> "The fruit of silence is Prayer,
>
> The fruit of prayer is Faith,
>
> The fruit of faith is Love,
>
> The fruit of love is Service,
>
> The fruit of service is Peace."

Prayer is meditating God's words in silence, and nobody can learn to know and understand God unless he or she prays. Prayer is the way to listen to God, to speak with Him, and to understand His love for us. Prayer not only helps to understand God, it also helps to understand ourselves, and as God is present in each one of us, prayer can help us to love one another. Prayer makes your heart bigger. If you pray with words, let them be filled with love and let your heart speak; you will then find joy in praying. Feel often during the day the need for prayer, and pray. From the very beginning, the Missionaries of Charity has been a praying community. They pray at home, on the street, and even during work, and every evening they have an hour of 'adoration', staying

"Please don't destroy the child; we'll take the child"

in God's presence in contemplation. His words help them to see His will for them. The Society celebrates the 7th of October every year, its foundation day, as Our Ladies Feast, and considers their being able to serve the poor as the fruit of their prayers. In keeping with the local traditions of Calcutta, where the Mission was founded, the Sisters of the Missionaries of Charity take their sandals off before going into the chapel, and kneel and sit on the floor.

Above every crucifix in all the homes of the Missionaries of Charity are the words "I Thirst," the words that Jesus spoke when He was dying on the cross. According to Mother Teresa, it was Jesus' thirst for our love, a thirst that is there in every one of us, rich and poor alike. Jesus died on the cross because that is what it took of Him to do good to us — to save us from our sins. He gave up His life in that way to do the Father's will, to show us that we too must be willing to give up everything to do God's will — to love one another as He loves each one of us. *This is the meaning of true love, to give until it hurts.*

In her speech at The National Prayer Breakfast at Washington DC, sponsored jointly by the US Senate and the House of Representatives in February 1994, Mother Teresa narrated one of her experiences. On hearing from someone that this Hindu family has had nothing

to eat for a long time, Mother immediately rushed there with some rice, and she saw hunger in the children's eyes. But, on receiving the rice, the mother of that house went out. When she came back, Mother asked her where she had been, and she was dumbstruck to hear that she had gone out to give that rice to a Muslim family, because "they are also hungry." *That mother gave even when it hurt her.*

In her address accepting the Nobel Peace Prize in 1979, Mother Teresa narrated two other such experiences in her life. One happened in Calcutta, where in the middle of a shortage in sugar, a four-year-old Hindu boy stopped eating sugar for three days and brought it to Mother to share it with the inmates of her home. The other took place probably in New York, where a man who had been bedridden for twenty years, and whose only pleasure had been his smoking, gave Mother $15, which he saved by not smoking for a week. *It must have hurt him too.* It is these types of gifts that filled her heart, and Mother always acknowledged that it would not have been possible for her to do what she has done without the prayers, gifts and continuous giving of all who donated to the Missionaries of Charity, and thanked whoever gave whatever they could. She would proclaim 'I don't want you to give me from your abundance, I want you to give until it hurts.'

Mother Teresa reminded every one that at the end of life, people will not be judged by how many diplomas they have received or how much money they have made, but by what "You Did It To Me," whether you gave Me to eat when I was hungry, clothe Me when I was naked, and took Me in when I was homeless. Hungry not only for bread, but also for love; Naked not only of clothing, but also for human dignity and respect; and homeless not for want of a roof over the head, but because of rejection. And, she would go on to say that on the last day, Jesus will say to those on His right, 'Come, enter the Kingdom, for you gave me food when I was hungry, drink when I was thirsty, and visited me when I was sick.' Then Jesus will turn to those on His left and say, 'Depart from me because you did not feed me when I was hungry, gave me to drink when I was thirsty, and did not visit me when I was sick.' These will then ask Him, 'When did we see You hungry or thirsty, or sick and did not come to your help?' And Jesus will answer, 'Whatever you neglected to do unto one of the least of these, you neglected to do unto Me.'

Mother Teresa was a strong advocate of love beginning at home, and reminded all concerned that 'the future of humanity passes through the family.' She advised people to start to love and serve their family first, and then to proceed with one's neighbourhood

before venturing further. She asked everyone to find the 'poor' in his or her family, and to love and serve them. She would point out that it may be possible that we have somebody in our own family who is feeling lonely, sick, or is worried, and we may not be by their side when they need us. In her speech to the US Senators and Congressmen at the National Prayer Breakfast in February 1994, Mother drew their attention to two varied experiences that she had in the West. One was a visit to a home, where they kept the old people whose children had put them there. The home had every comfort available, but Mother did not find a single inmate with a smile on his or her face and found all of them looking expectantly towards the door. On enquiring from the Sister there, Mother came to know that everyday the inmates would watch the door expecting a son or a daughter to come and visit them, but no one came. They were hurt because they were forgotten.

The other was Mother's shock in finding out why so many young girls and boys in the West had given in to drugs. She found that often the parents were too busy, or they were not married or had broken up since, and so there was no one in the family to give them attention — as a result of which these children take to the streets and get involved in drugs. Thus, Mother Teresa saw both sides of the shining coin, and found the emotional poverty of the

West much more difficult to remove. Mother said that the hunger of a person could be satisfied and removed by giving him a plate of rice or a piece of bread, but it is difficult to remove the poverty of someone who feels unwanted or unloved. She observed that in the developed countries there is a poverty of intimacy, a poverty of spirit, of loneliness and of lack of love, and considered this the greatest sickness that the world is facing today.

The accomplishments of Mother Teresa's life are enormous. She established homes for unwanted babies and children, created colonies for lepers, and set up dwellings where people could die with dignity. Her Missionaries of Charity, members of which congregation, besides taking the three basic vows of poverty, chastity and obedience, take the fourth vow of serving the poorest of the poor, are present in 105 countries across the globe and to quote Mother herself, 'If there are poor on the moon, we will go there too.' Today the Society has 570 missions around the world, comprising 4,000 nuns, a brotherhood of 300, and over 1,00,000 lay volunteers operating homes for AIDS, leprosy and tuberculosis patients, soup kitchens, counseling programmes for children and families, orphanages and schools.

Whether it was feeding the hungry in Ethiopia, serving the poor in the ghettos of South Africa, rescuing trapped sick children at the height of the siege in Beirut, caring for the millions of refugees from Bangladesh, taking care of the radiation victims in Chernobyl, or giving succor to the people of her native Albania when the communist regime collapsed, Calcutta's Mother Teresa, *the living Saint*, was always present. Mother Teresa became a symbol of untiring commitment to the poor and the suffering.

Together with all this work, Mother Teresa was known all over the world as the staunchest opponent of abortion. She fought relentlessly against abortion, and would go about pleading with clinics, hospitals and police stations not to destroy the child, and to hand it over to her; and she would usher in unwed mothers, take care of the mother and child and find a home for the child. She considered abortion the most heinous form of murder, and the greatest destroyer of peace, 'because it is a direct war, direct killing, direct murder by the mother herself,' and continued, 'if a mother can kill her own child, what is left for me to kill you, and you to kill me.' She advocated the right of the unborn child to live, and considered it a crime to decide that an unborn child must die because She defended the right to life of everyone, especially that of the unborn, because whereas adults are capable of taking decisions about themselves, children and the child yet to be born were incapable of doing so. Adults are adults because they know the possible consequences of their acts, and so Mother concluded that if people decide to make love, they know that this could lead to the birth of a child; and if that happens, then the child should be accepted as a fruit of their love, a gift of God. To her, love of the child is where love and peace began. Even in her speech at Oslo, accepting the Nobel Peace Prize in 1979, she boldly proclaimed that all those who were present there were there because their parents loved them and wanted them, and called on them to love their children, and to want them in turn.

Mother considered countries that allow abortion as cowards, not having the courage to accept one more life. In a now famous letter to the US Supreme Court, she reminded the Court of those words of the Declaration of

Independence which always stirred the human heart everywhere, "We hold these truths to be self evident: that all men are *created* equal; that they are endowed by their *creator* with certain inalienable rights; that among these are *life*, liberty, and the pursuit of happiness...," and argued that if the right to life is inalienable, then it must surely exist wherever life *exists*. She continued that 'no one can deny that the unborn child is a distinct being, that it is human, and that it is alive,' and, therefore it is unjust to deprive the unborn child of its fundamental right to life on the basis of its age, size, or condition of dependency.

She criticised the court's decision to exclude the unborn child from the human family and its ruling that a mother has discretion to choose to destroy the unborn child. She commented that it was a sad infidelity to America's highest ideals when its Supreme Court observed that it did not matter or could not be determined, when the inalienable right to life began for a child in its mother's womb. She warned that this decision aggravated the derogation of the father's role in an increasingly fatherless society as it portrayed the greatest gift of God, the child, as a competitor, an intrusion and an inconvenience; and nominally accorded mothers unfettered domination over the independent lives of their physically dependent children. In granting this unjustified power, it has exposed women to unjust and selfish demands of their husbands or other sexual partners.

She had strongly worded the ending of that letter, and wrote that human rights are not a privilege conferred by government, but an entitlement by virtue of humanity, and the right to life does not depend, and must not be declared to be contingent on the pleasure of anyone else, not even a parent or a sovereign. She rightly alleged that the Court's decision has sown violence and discord at the heart of the most intimate human relationship.

In her speech accepting the Nobel Prize, she announced that the Missionaries of Charity was fighting abortion by adoption, and pleaded, "Please don't destroy the child; we will take the child." She explained that while it was true that there are quite a number of unwed mothers, it was also true that there was a tremendous demand for children from families who have no children. She contended that many people were concerned with the increasing number of deaths of children in India and Africa from malnutrition, hunger and diseases, but were not as bothered with the millions of children dying due to the deliberate will of the mother.

In continuation of her belief that adults indulge in acts of love and that a child is the greatest gift of God, Mother Teresa advocated natural family planning as against chemical contraception.

Since natural family planning needs the cooperation, consent and indulgence of both partners, this inculcates responsible behaviour of the adults. According to her, taking such resposibility of one another, and of life as such, teaches an attitude of mutual attention resulting in love and forgivenness. Although motherhood is a special gift of God to women, the child is God's best gift to the entire family and needs both mother and father, because each one shows God's love in a special way. When families are broken or disunited, many children grow up not knowing how to love. A country with many such broken families has many problems, but in a country of strong and united families, children grow up as loving and caring citizens. Love begins at home — in our families, in our community, and peace emanates from love. Works of love are always works of peace.

CHAPTER FOUR

Moments Of God

Mother Teresa often told those who came to her willing to serve the poor as she did, "What I can do, you cannot. What you can do, I cannot. But together we can do something beautiful for God."

The society of the Missionaries of Charity has eight branches. Each one of them originated as and when the situation arose, and is assigned a different purpose. The first were the Active Sisters, started in 1950, and the contemplative sisters or the *Sisters of the World* came into being in 1976. The sisters of both these branches take the four vows of obedience, charity, chastity and free and unconditional service to the poorest of the poor. They had to undergo a rigorous training for six years.

Once the Active Sisters started their work, very soon some young men started helping Mother Teresa to bring in the sick people from the streets, carry heavy weights and go out at night. Many of these young men wanted to devote their life in the service of the poor. This is how the congregation of the *Brothers Missionaries of Charity* started. Here also, as the need arose, *an active* and a *contemplative* branch were born. In the middle of 1980, some priests in America expressed the desire to live according to the spirituality and rule of the Missionaries

'The Fruit of Prayer is Faith'

of Charity. This started as the Corpus Christi movement, and was the forerunner of the *Fathers Missionaries of Charity*. They have a novicate in Rome, where boys and men desiring to become priests under the Missionaries of Charity get their religious training.

It was in 1985-86 in Italy, Belgium and France that common people who wanted to serve the cause of the Missionaries of Charity from outside the Church organised themselves and Mother Teresa asked Father Sebastian to be their spiritual leader. However, it was only in 1988/89 that the *Lay Missionaries* received their name and had their first constitution. The Lay Missionaries wear ordinary clothes, but carry a cross on their left shoulder, and assist the sisters in their work all over the world. They lead a life of poverty and devotion, and are at close tandem with the spirit of the Missionaries of Charity. The volunteers helping the Sisters of the Missionaries of Charity have always been there since its very inception. These are young people, and other socially or religiously inspired people who help the sisters all over the world. They help mostly for short durations and are assigned specific jobs for the duration that they want to help in the Society's work.

When Sister Teresa left the Loreto convent and went to Patna to get training in nursing, she met there a young Belgian, Jacqueline

1894 - 1995

Souvenir

SACRED HEART

De Decker, sociologist and nurse by training and working with the poor in Madras. She expressed her desire to start working with Mother. However, her health soon broke down and she was forced to go back to Belgium, where the doctors discovered that she had a serious disease of the spine, and soon it was known that she would never be able to go back to India to work with Mother. Then Mother Teresa wrote to her asking her to be the Suffering link between the Sisters of the Missionaries of Charity and the sick from all over the world. Jacqueline accepted Mother's advice, and thus in January 1953 the *Sick and the Suffering Co-workers* started. For every sister of the Society, there was a suffering link, and they wrote to each other once a year. Jacqueline became a link between the Sisters and the sick. Mother Teresa called them 'the Power House of the MC.'

An English lady, Ann Blaike met Mother Teresa in Calcutta in 1954 and helped Mother with her "Touch a leper with your compassion" campaign. This lady returned to England in 1960 and started to coordinate with like-minded people in Europe who were interested in the work of Mother Teresa, and it was in 1969 that she worked with Mother Teresa in Rome on the constitution of the *International Association of the Co-workers of Mother Teresa*. Mother Teresa defined a co-worker as someone who would work continuously to share the tiredness, the humiliation, and the shame of someone else, and wanted them to be the fire of love among the poor, the sick, the dying and the little children.

While most of the Co-Workers were sincere people, eager to help and devote themselves to the service of the poorest of the poor, some among them tried to take advantage of the name of Mother Teresa. They started fund raising through all kinds of commercial activities in her name. So, on 22nd July 1994, Mother decided to put an end to this chapter, but allowed those who wanted to, to continue helping the Sisters in their service as Volunteers.

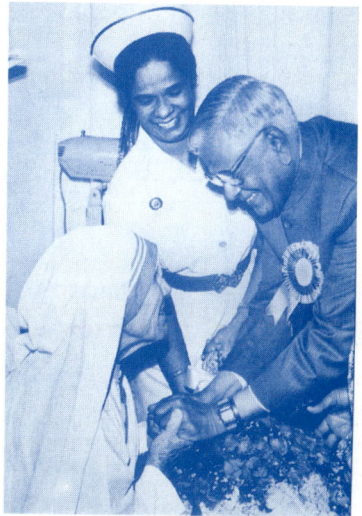

With the then President of India
R. Venkataraman

As far as material means were concerned, Mother Teresa depended on divine providence. Mother did not mind asking for money, kindness, to give shape to her projects for the poorest of the poor; whenever she needed a special favour, she would indulge in a Litany or a Novena, but she was strongly against any sort of commercial activities for fund raising for her cause. She believed that she was answerable to Jesus for every *paisa* that people gave her, every word she spoke, and for every action of her's. She would say that the only thing she was afraid of was money, the greed and the love of money, for that is what had motivated Judas to betray Jesus.

One of Mother Teresa's first recollections of God approving her service to the poorest of the poor was in her very early years, when one day a man she did not know came to her shack and gave her an envelope containing fifty rupees for her work. This happened just after she had given her last rupee as a contribution to some worthy project. Then there was that small boy who gave up eating sugar to give it to Mother, the man who gave up smoking for a week to save money to give to Mother, and many such acts of 'love till it hurts.' And this did not happen only in India, but throughout the world. Mother would say that in giving, there is nothing small; the moment something is given to God, it becomes infinite. It is the love behind the deed that makes it great.

Later on in her life, pharmaceutical companies gave her medicines, shop owners gave her food and clothing, millionaires wrote out hefty cheques, and powerful heads of corporate houses, and even states and countries donated land, buildings, money and food. And Mother would tell them, 'it is not how much we do, but how much love we put in the doing; it is not how much we give, but how much love we put in the giving.' Once a chairman of a multinational company came to see Mother and offered her a property in Bombay. During the course of his interaction with Mother, he asked her how she managed her budget. Mother in turn asked back as to who had sent him to her. The gentleman replied, 'I felt an urge inside me,' and Mother told him that other people also came to her and said the same thing. She told him that this indicated that God had sent him, as He sends the others who provide the material means needed to render service to the poor; thus he was her 'budget'.

God's love in action

Mother gave all that she received to her cause, and she never missed an opportunity to encash a situation for her cause. The cash award that came with the Nobel Prize, which she received 'in the name of the hungry, the naked, the homeless, of the crippled, of the blind, of the lepers, of all those who feel unwanted, unloved, uncared for throughout society, people that have become a burden to the society and are shunned by everyone', and from other prizes and awards was used to make homes for many who had none. She requested the dinner scheduled to be held there in her honour to be cancelled and the $6,000 thus saved to be given to her to 'feed 400 poor children for a year in India'. Similarly, when Pope Paul VI came to India in 1964, he gave Mother his ceremonial limousine, which she immediately raffled to help finance her leper colony.

Mother considered serving the poorest of the poor as her tryst with Christ, and her moments spent with them as *moments of love*, the moments when she virtually felt God's grace passing through her. Mother realised one such 'moment' in the very beginning of starting her work when she had picked up a dying woman from the street, her face half eaten by rodents and insects, and took her to a place where she could die with dignity. She died with a smile on her face. Another time was when the sisters picked up a man, half-eaten by worms, from the drain and brought him to the home for the dying. They cleaned him and put him on a neat bed, and the man said, 'I have lived like an animal in the street, but I am going to die like an angel, loved and cared for. Sister, I am going home to God'. Similarly, when she touched the smelling body of a leper, she would feel as if she was touching Christ himself.

Mother Teresa considered herself as '*a pencil in God's hands.*' She always searched for what God wanted her to do, rather than what she wanted to do. She looked for God's will in her actions, His direction for her actions.

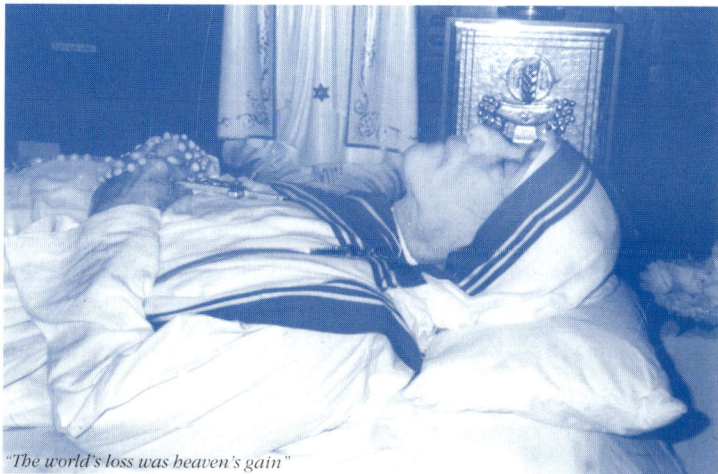

"The world's loss was heaven's gain"

CHAPTER FIVE

A Star Is Born

Mother Teresa once said that if not for anything else she will be going to heaven for all the publicity, which has actually purified her and sacrificed her, and readied her to go to heaven.

While most people spoke highly about Mother Teresa, there were small murmurings of dissent too. Whereas Evangelist Billy Graham would remember his meeting her as 'meeting a saint,' and many others agreed with him, Christopher Hitchens had his personal view that while Mother preached obedience and resignation to the poor, she had consoled and supported the rich and powerful, allowing them all manner of indulgence.

Her relentless and continued service to the poorest of the poor in their environment, her travels all over the world, and her growing years had its toll on Mother's health. She had her first heart attack

With Pope John Paul II

in 1985 when she was 75 and visiting Pope John Paul II in Rome. Another, almost fatal, heart attack occurred in 1989, and a pacemaker had to be implanted. While visiting Tijuana in Mexico in 1991, she suffered from a bout of pneumonia, which resulted in another episode of heart failure.

It was due to her failing health that Mother Teresa announced her resignation in August 1990, forty years after she set up the Missionaries of Charity. However, the conclave of sisters, who were to choose a successor to Mother in a secret ballot, voted unanimously for Mother to continue, the only dissenting vote being that of Mother herself. Mother heeded to their request, and withdrew her resignation. But her health remained indifferent. In 1996, after a brief spell of chest infection coupled with malaria, she had to undergo heart surgery once again. This time the sisters understood her plea to be relieved, and on March 13th 1997, the assembly of sisters elected Sister Nirmala as the new Superior General to continue Mother's work.

On September 5, 1997 at around 9.30 pm, the lamp of Mother's earthly life finally burnt out from her wholehearted and unconditional giving of herself to the service of the poorest of the poor. Mother Teresa died in Mother's House in Calcutta, and was

"If it is not of God, it will die out, if it is of God it will last"

united with her Christ in heaven. The teacher who taught love for humanity to mankind was no more. The world's loss was heaven's gain. A star was born.

Mother Teresa's body was laid out in state and thousands came to pay homage — standing in queue for hours, carrying handfuls of flowers. Her funeral took place on September 13th, 1997.

Mother Teresa was given a state funeral in Calcutta in the presence of queens, first ladies, presidents, prime ministers, former heads of states from over 23 countries across the world and religious leaders of all faiths. The gun carriage that had pulled the casket of Mahatma Gandhi in 1948 was once again put in service to do the honours for Mother Teresa, and the funeral services was led by Cardinal A. Sodano, the pontiff's representative. The funeral represented some beautiful symbolism of the various aspects of Mother's work and in the presence of world leaders, the elite of the society and the inmates of the various homes of the Missionaries of Charity, the 'presentation of the gifts' were made by a handicapped orphan, a leper, a woman released from prison, a retarded boy and a sister of the Missionaries of Charity.

On hearing the news of Mother Teresa's death, Jacques Chirac, the French Prime Minister, observed, "Tonight there is less love, less compassion, less light in the world," and in his condolence message, Pope John Paul II referred to Mother as "a woman who has left her mark on the history of this century." Queen Elizabeth wrote, "Mother Teresa will continue to live in the hearts of all those who have been touched by her selfless work," while South African President Nelson Mandela put it as "a loss to the entire humanity," and the Malaysian Prime Minister Mahathir Mohamed described Mother Teresa as "an example of selfless devotion to charity." The Russian President Boris Yeltsin remarked, "Mother Teresa will always remain in the hearts and minds of Russians as a friend of our country, ready to render help at any moment." Henry D'Souza, the then Archbishop of Calcutta said, "Perhaps the greatest message she has given is the value of dignity of human life, that all human life is precious," while Archbishop Charles J. Chaput, Archdiocese of Denver, commented that "Mother Teresa's life proved that the only real revolution in human affairs flows from service to others."

'United with Christ in Heaven' — *Cemetery of Mother Teresa*

At a mass to commemorate Mother Teresa's passing away, Jaime Cardinal Sin of the Philippines observed, "We are here to grieve the loss of a precious jewel, a glorious crown and a golden heart in the Church." Archbishop Francis George, the Archdiocese of Chicago observed, "Mother Teresa spent her life with the Lord, especially serving Him in the poor, and she must be happy to meet Him face to face now," and Bishop David E. Foley, Diocese of Birmingham, Alabama, revered, "the passing of Mother Teresa is a moment of joy because of her holiness; we are happy to offer to God such a lovely soul."

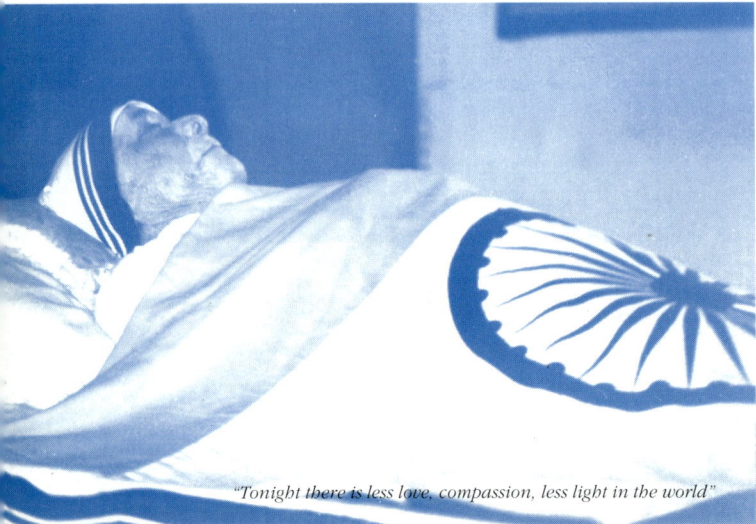

"Tonight there is less love, compassion, less light in the world"

There was mourning all over the world, and people bowed their heads in reverence to Mother Teresa, prayed, exchanged words of regret, and ultimately life started normalising after the funeral and burial on the 13th September. The truth that emanated was that Mother Teresa was no more. However, Sister Nirmala and the other sisters of the Missionaries of Charity could still feel Mother's presence.

The question that probably came to the minds of many people then was, 'will the Missionaries of Charity last after the death of Mother Teresa?' And the answer lay in the Bible itself where it said, "if it is not of God it will die out, if it is of God it will last". In Mother Teresa's words, "If you are humble nothing will touch you, neither praise nor disgrace, because you know what you are".

Life Line

1910   Born August 26, as Gonxha Bojaxhiu in Skopje, Yugoslavia (now Macedonia). Baptised on August 27, as Agnes Gonxha Bojaxhiu.

1919   Father expires when she is just 9.

1922   Desires to spend her life for God's work.

1928   Joins the Order of the Sisters of Our Lady of Loreto in Ireland.

1929   Reached her dream country — India.

1929-1948   Teaches at St. Mary's High School at Calcutta, of which she becomes the Principal in 1944.

1948   Leaves the convent to work with the "poorest of the poor", her "call within a call".

1950	Becomes a citizen of India. October 7, she receives permission from Pope Pius XII to start her own order. The Missionaries of Charity is founded.
1952	Nirmal Hriday, the house for the dying is established at Kalighat, Calcutta.
1953	Shishu Vihar, the first orphanage is set up in Calcutta.
1957	The Missionaries of Charity starts work with lepers. Establishes Shanti Nagar, the first village of lepers.
1962	Receives 'Padma Shri' for her "distinguished service" to humanity.
1965	Pope Paul VI grants Mother Teresa's request to expand globally.
1966	Missionaries of Charity Brothers founded.
1971	Pope Paul VI honours Mother Teresa with the first Pope John XXIII Peace Prize. Also receives the Boston Prize of the Good Samaritan and the Kennedy Prize.
1972	Receives the Jawaharlal Nehru Award for International Understanding from the President of India, who addresses her as *Koruna Dutt*, the angel of charity.
1973	Receives the Templeton Prize.
1979	Receives the Noble Prize for Peace.
1980	The Missionaries of Charity starts homes for drug addicts.
1982	Receives the Doctor Honoris Causa from the Catholic University, Brussels.

1985   President Reagan presents her the Medal of Freedom, the highest US civilian award. Suffers her first heart attack while visiting Pope John Paul II in Rome. The Missionaries of Charity establishes the first hospice for AIDS victims.

1989   Her second, almost fatal heart attack; pacemaker is implanted.

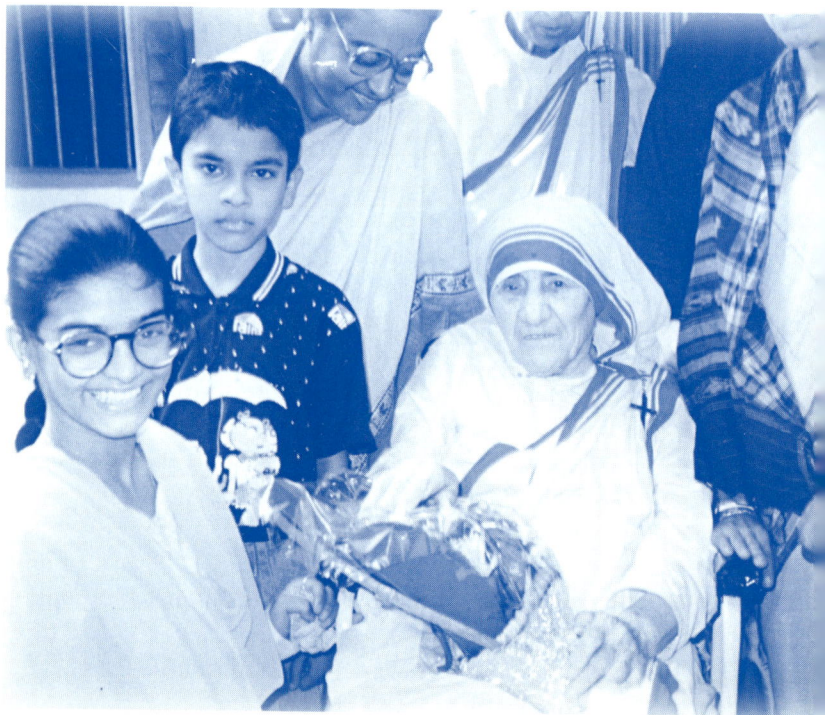

1990   August, Mother Teresa announces her resignation, but the conclave of sisters elects her once again. Withdraws resignation.

1991   Mother Teresa visits Albania (now known as Serbia) for the first time after leaving home in 1928. Suffers from pneumonia in Tijuana, Mexico, leads to heart failure.

1993   May, Breaks three ribs in a fall in Rome; August, hospitalised in New Delhi with malaria; September, undergoes heart surgery for blocked blood vessel in Calcutta.

1994   February 3rd, addresses National Prayer Breakfast sponsored jointly by the US Senate and the House of Representatives.

1996   Receives honorary US citizenship, only the fourth in the world to do so. Suffers malaria and chest infection and undergoes heart surgery.

1997   March 13, Sister Nirmala is elected as Mother Teresa's successor. On September 5, Mother Teresa dies at Mother House in Calcutta.

BIBLIOGRAHY

My Life For the Poor
—Mother Teresa

Mother Teresa — Navin Chawla

*Mahatma Gandhi, Mother Teresa,
Swami Vivekananda and Some
Important Events of India from
1941 to March 1995*
— Saroj Kanti Majumdar

*The Missionary Position:
Mother Teresa in Theory
and Practice*
— Christopher Hitchens

God bless you
M Teresa mc

67

NOTES